Study Guide:
Anchored in Christ,
Anchored in Marriage

La'Toya Guillory

ISBN-13: 978-1-7348397-1-5

TO MY READERS

I hope and pray that throughout this study you will feel the presence of God as He speaks to you. I encourage you to be open to hear what the Holy Spirit wants to reveal. Use this time to reflect. Let the words that are written be the starting point of a beautiful relationship with God. Allow Him to lead the way and remember to trust the process.

CONTENTS

Armor up

Are you ready for battle? Consider this; marriages are falling by the wayside because too few people have come prepared for the fight. Couples have either lost sight of who God is or never really knew Him in the first place. Your armor is essential for defeating the enemy at his schemes. He only has the power that we give him. The bible tells us that God will do exceedingly and abundantly above all we ask or think according to the power that works within us (Ephesians 3:20 NASB).

Most people apply that scripture to monetary things, but I believe that it can apply to many areas of our lives. I've used it when completing coursework for graduate school, applying for jobs, believing for breakthroughs for family and friends. I've even used it in my own marriage, during tough seasons. This scripture has gotten me through a lot.

I don't know who you are or what you're going through. What I do know is that God wants to fulfill that scripture in your life. He wants you to have a fruitful marriage. It's time to remind the enemy who you are! Your spouse does not belong to him, your children don't belong to him, your finances don't belong to him, and your family does not belong to him. It's time for war, folks!!!

"Be well balanced (temperate, sober mind), be vigilant and cautious at all times; for that enemy of yours, the devil, roams around like a lion roaring [in fierce hunger], seeking someone to seize upon and devour."

- 1 Peter 5:8-9 (AMPC)

Introduction

There is a real enemy out there that who is looking for someone to devour. He prowls around like a roaring lion to see who he can destroy. Not only must we be alert to win this fight, we must stay alert. He will try anything and everything to ruin your family dynamic. Don't let him. My prayer is that as you read through "Anchored" while using this study guide so that you will learn to stand firm during the most challenging battles in your relationship. See, the enemy has one job to do on this earth. That is to destroy it. He can only do what he was created to do.

God, on the other hand, wants to do the opposite. He created you and your spouse for a purpose. His job is to walk out this thing called life with you. He is fighting for you every step of the way. The truth is that the fight is already won. Jesus defeated our enemy on the cross. Our job is to remain steadfast in Him, to stay unshakeable when we want to throw in the towel. It's our job to remain anchored, fixed in one place. If you are in a marriage that God has not called you to, or if your relationship has become dangerous, then this study guide is not for you. If you want to enhance your marriage. If you want the tools to maintain a healthy marriage, keep reading. As you work through this study guide, you will see two sections to assist you on this journey.

Heart Check

This section discusses the main points of the book and draws you deeper. This section also assists you in applying scriptures to different areas of your relationship. It also allows you to check the areas of your heart that are hindering you from moving forward. The questions in this section will be both reflective and informative.

War Cry

This section prompts us to surrender we acknowledged above everything to God that. After it is released, you will have a time of reflection.

Chapter 1

Complete Surrender

Read the heart check section along with chapter one of Anchored before answering the questions below.

In my profession, I often notice that people will react to a situation before responding. When we do this, we lose sight of the scripture in James 1:19 (NIV);

"My dear brothers and sisters, take note of this: Everyone should be quick to listen, slow to speak, and slow to become angry."

When we apply this scripture to our lives, it allows us to hear from the Holy Spirit first before we react to a situation negatively.

1. In your own words, describe what being married means to you?

    _____

    _____

    _____

_____

_____

2. Is what you described what you are living right now? Why or why not?

_____

_____

_____

_____

_____

3. Do you believe you and your spouse have a healthy view of marriage? Why or Why not? If the answer is yes, what did it take for you to get to that place?

_____

_____

_____

_____

_____

"Marriage is a daily surrender. It will show you how selfish you really are. It will show you how much you must depend on God for direction. To remain anchored, you must die to your own selfish ambitions."

4. List areas of your life that bring out your selfish side. What are some things that you can do to be more compassionate and empathetic in these areas of your life?

_____

_____

_____

_____

_____

"A person standing alone can be attacked and defeated, but two can stand back-to-back and conquer. Three are even better, for a triple braided cord is not easily broken."   *-Eccl. 4:12 (NIV)*

"To remain anchored, your vision for your family must outweigh your own bitterness and unforgiveness."

5. What areas of your life or relationship are you refusing to let God touch? Is there anything in your life that you feel is too hard to let go?

_____

_____

_____

_____

_____

Surrender is a big word. To completely surrender anything in your life means you must let go of control. It means that you must get out of the driver's seat and let God take the wheel.

In chapter one of my book, we discussed the story of Abraham and Sarah. If you are not familiar with the story, God promised Abraham and Sarah that not only would Abraham be a father in his old age, but he would be the father of many nations. After he received his promise, God asked Abraham to sacrifice their son. Though it didn't make sense to Abraham, he remained obedient to God and decided to sacrifice their son. In true God form, God provided a sacrificial ram in Isaac's place. Abraham was fully committed to carrying out the task. He believed that God would provide a way to keep Isaac alive. He knew that God was in control. Abraham believed that God's promises are "yes" and "amen" even when it didn't make sense.

6. Generational curses are real. Take a moment to think about your childhood. Now compare your personal struggles to any struggles that you witnessed in your family. Do you notice any similarities? List them here.

_____

_____

_____

_____

_____

"It takes true sacrifice to say, "Lord, I give it all to you. My doubts, my worries, my fears, my marriage, my finances, my job, my health, my purpose, and my children". That is exactly what faith is. It is relying on what you can't see and allowing God to do the rest.

War Cry

Lord, make me over again. Renew a right spirit within me. The heart is deceitful above all things according to your word. I surrender my heart and mind to you right now. Remove all malice, bitterness, and every other spirit that is hindering my relationship with you. Restore everything that was stolen from me and freely given. Let your love saturate my heart. Wrap your loving arms around me. Have your way in me. In Jesus' name.
Amen.

Scripture Study:

Matthew 6:33, James 4:7, Matthew 11:28, Proverbs 23:26, Matthew

26:3

Chapter 2

Inner Healing

Read chapter two of Anchored before answering the questions below.

1. Describe your thoughts toward God. How do you see Him?
   What do you believe are His character traits? Be honest with
   yourself. No one is here to judge you. God already knows how
   you feel. He is waiting for you to acknowledge these feelings.

   _____

   _____

   _____

   _____

   _____

*"Then Jesus said, Come to Me, all of you, who are weary and carry
heavy burdens, and I will give you rest. Take My yoke upon you. Let
Me teach you because I am humble and gentle at heart, and you will
find rest for your souls. For My yoke is easy to bear, and My burden is
light." – Matthew 11:28-30*

**"Most people feel as though you have to clean yourself up to
come to Him. The truth is you don't put clean clothes in a washing**

machine. If you do, you wasted your money because the washing machine can't do its job. We cannot clean ourselves up. That is God's job. By doing so, we stifle His ability to show us Himself. Our job is to completely surrender to Him and allow Him to lead and guide us into His truth. It's in complete surrender that inner healing can take place."

2. Are there situations that have happened in your life that cause you to operate in fear, anger, resentment, bitterness, hate, anxiety, or depression? If so, are you ready to release them to God? When we release them, God can restore us and restore our marriages as well.

_____

_____

_____

_____

_____

Freedom, that's what God gives us when we acknowledge He exists. When we recognize that He is everything we need Him to be. The struggles we have been living with become His. God takes our brokenness and puts us back together again. We begin to live Galatians 5:22-23, which says,

"But the fruit of the spirit is love, joy, peace, forbearance, kindness, goodness, faithfulness, gentleness, and self-control. Against such things, there is no law." (NIV)

Saying the "word" freedom and seeing it on paper is entirely different from experiencing it. There is something about the freedom of God that is unexplainable. His freedom brings about His peace. It brings about the fruits of His spirit. It gives us an understanding of who we are and who's we are.

3. What does freedom mean to you? How does it make you feel when you see the word "freedom"? Do you believe that the freedom you have in God is attainable in your life?

    _____

    _____

    _____

    _____

    _____

"Now to Him who is able to [carry out His purpose and] do superabundantly more than all that we dare ask or think [infinitely beyond our greatest prayers, hopes, or dreams], according to His power that is at work within us."

Ephesians 3:20 (AMP)

You are God's masterpiece. Think about that. The Mona Lisa cannot compete with you in God's eyes. There is nothing that can separate us from the love of God. Whether you like it or not, there is nothing you can do to change it. Now that doesn't mean that He doesn't want a relationship with you. It just means that His love is unconditional.

You may feel like you've messed up and God could never love you after the things you've done. BUT GOD! There is nothing you can do or say that can make Him stop loving you. Of course, this isn't an excuse for you to do things that are not good for you. You don't want to dig yourself in a deeper hole. What it means is that God wants to do a new thing in your life. Inner healing allows God to take your heart and remove the clogs that cause it to beat irregularly.

4. Are there people in your life that you have not forgiven for past hurts? If yes, call them out by name and release them to God. If it helps, use this space to write their names out.

_____

_____

_____

_____

_____

"One of the hardest things to do in this lifetime is to forgive. Am I right? I find it so difficult to forgive someone when I feel wronged in any kind of way. I know that people aren't as forthcoming as I can be, but the truth of the matter is that I'm not alone in this. It takes a lot of energy to hold on to unforgiveness, even for the most gruesome act. My challenge for all of us is to forgive anyway. Forgive them even if it doesn't make sense."

5. If you listed anyone in the previous section, take this time to pray for them. Forgiveness does not mean that you excuse what happened. It means that you surrender it to God and let Him have His way with it.

"As if forgiveness isn't hard enough, your true test of being set free is in the way you love."

Jesus loved beyond His comfort zone. Even as His people crucified Him, He prayed for them. He invited them to partake in God's goodness.

6. Chapter 2 of Anchored discusses the love chapter in 1 Corinthians 13:4-8 (NIV). I encourage you to insert your name everywhere that love is. If you struggle in this area, ask God to help you get through it.

4 _____ is patient, _____ is kind. _____ does not envy, _____ does not boast, _____ is not proud. 5 _____ does not dishonor others, _____ is not self-seeking, _____ is not easily angered, _____ keeps no record of wrongs. 6 _____ does not delight in evil but rejoices with the truth. 7 ____ always protects, always trusts, always hopes, always perseveres. 8 _____ never fails. But where there are prophecies, they will cease; where there are tongues, they will be stilled; where there is knowledge, it will pass away.

"Freedom is such a peaceful feeling. For your inner healing to take root, we have to come to an understanding that we are free."

The enemy knows you just like God does. He knows what can take you off course and how to cause arguments in your home. He also knows how to keep you from your purpose. Don't worry. God is on your side. He is ready for any and everything the enemy throws your way.

War Cry

Lord, I need you like never before. I want a life of freedom not just for myself, but also for my family. Create in me a clean heart. In Jesus' name. Amen.

Scripture Study

Psalm 147:3, Jeremiah 30:17, Psalm 142:7, Psalm 30:2,

Psalm 34:18

Chapter 3

I Choose you

Read chapter three of Anchored before answering the questions in this section.

"If you are reading this and have taken my advice, a lot has taken place in your life up to this point. This chapter is all about making a choice. By now, you have chosen to surrender to God completely, and some inner healing has taken place. Now it's time to choose. "

1. Look at yourself through your spouse's eyes. Put yourself in their shoes. Are there choices you made that could have been handled differently? What would you have done otherwise?

    _____

    _____

    _____

    _____

    _____

2. If you have wronged your spouse in any way, own it, apologize, and ask for their forgiveness. Remember that we cannot expect perfection from our spouses, knowing that we are not perfect. The same grace that was given to us at the cross has been given to our spouses as well. (Pause and reflect on this.)

Marriage is a sanctity between two people. In other words, other people's opinions don't matter. You have to be in agreement with your spouse. We also need to understand that if our relationship is unhealthy or even toxic, the right counselors are available to you. While some relationships can get better with counseling, others may not.

3. In what ways have you allowed other people's opinions to influence decisions in your marriage?

_____

_____

_____

_____

_____

We do not need to have all the answers to life's problems, but we can choose to look up. God invented relationships. He even wants to have a relationship with us. God walks with us, talks with us, and shows us where He wants us to go. When we choose Him, He gives us the

wisdom we need to overcome every obstacle that we encounter in our

lifetime.

War Cry

Lord, I have not made all the right choices in my life, but I thank you that you are guiding me on the right path. You have always chosen me, and I am eternally grateful. I thank you that you are giving me eyes to see and ears to hear your truth. Have your way in me. In Jesus' name.
Amen.

Scripture Study

2 Peter 3:9, 2 Chronicles 9:7, Proverbs 16:9, Revelation 3:20

Chapter 4

A New Beginning

Read Chapter four before answering the questions below.

"'Every day has a new beginning, a new blessing, and a new hope'" (Anonymous). With this understanding, we can embrace this journey called life, without doubt, worry, or fear, knowing that if we do fail, God will be right there to dust us off so we can try again."

1. What fears have you allowed in your life to prevent you from moving forward into your destiny?

   _____

   _____

   _____

   _____

   _____

2. What has God called you to do that you do not feel confident in accomplishing?

   _____

   _____

   _____

_____

_____

Moses didn't need Aaron to complete the task that God asked him to do. He was capable of completing the assignment on his own. God fulfilled his request and used Aaron to help Moses gain the confidence he needed. I can admit that leading a large group of people into the promised land is pretty scary.

What I love about this story is that God knew precisely what Moses needed to lead them. I also love that even though Moses didn't see the promised land, God raised up someone else under his leadership to pass the baton to. He was not only determined to make Moses a leader. He was determined to allow Moses to leave a legacy for years to come. Through Moses' and Joshua's obedience, the children of Israel made it to the promised land.

Obedience builds faith. It's not about following rules; it's about taking God at His word to complete the task that He gives you.

3. Are there areas of your life where you have taken on the Moses complex? If so, Why?

_____

_____

_____

_____

_____

In our house, we have a saying," teamwork makes the dream work." Marriage is not a competition. We all have to work together to accomplish our goals. Of course, we have disagreements, but we make a point to get through them.

4. Are there areas of your relationship that you feel would be better if you worked together? If so, have a discussion with your spouse about it.
   What was the outcome of this discussion?

   _____

   _____

   _____

   _____

   _____

5. What area(s) of your relationship do you need to surrender to the Holy Spirit?

   _____

   _____

   _____

_____

_____

New beginnings can be scary but remember that the enemy knows your

capabilities. The irony of it all is that he is terrified of us. He knows the

purposes and plans that God has for us, so he will distort them and cause

us to revert back to our old ways. The enemy will only do what we allow

him to do. We must remember that God knows us too. We have to

remain focused and trust the process.

War Cry

**Lord, I know that I am treading in new territory, but I trust
you. Help me to stay focused on you as you lead me to my promised
land. I know that it won't be easy, but I am determined to trust the
process. In Jesus' name.
Amen.**

Scripture Study

2 Corinthians 4:16-17, 2 Corinthians 5:17,

Isaiah 43:18-19

Chapter 5

Pursuing your Passions

Read Chapter five of Anchored before answering the questions below.

"Some of you may be asking, 'Why would God use me for anything? Maybe it's hard for you to feel like you have a purpose, but the truth is we all have a purpose, whether we see it or not. Purpose is only our passions fulfilled."

1. What are you passionate about?

_____

_____

_____

_____

_____

Our passions should bring about the fruits of the Holy Spirit that

we talked about earlier in Galatians 5:22-23. Let's take another look at it

in the amplified version.

"But the fruit of the Spirit [the result of His presence within us] is love [unselfish concern for others], joy, [inner] peace, patience [not the ability to wait, but how we act while waiting], kindness, goodness, faithfulness, gentleness, self-control. Against such things, there is no law."

2. If you believe you have found your purpose, are the fruits of the spirit evident in your life? If not, be honest with where you are and allow God to point you in the right direction.

_____

_____

_____

_____

_____

As you may have heard, self-care is essential. Often, in relationships, we tend to lose our identity, we put our passions and purpose on the back burner. We find it hard to balance parenthood and career. We forget that God has assigned a task to all of us that will not go away. You are not your spouse. Your assignment may be different from theirs, but God will show you how to bring it all together.

3. If you have not done so already, discuss your passions with your spouse. Discuss your purpose with each other and begin to work together to see them fulfilled.

What was the outcome of this discussion?

_____

_____

_____

_____

_____

"For You formed my innermost parts; You knit me [together] in my mother's womb. I will give thanks and praise to You, for I am fearfully and wonderfully made; wonderful are Your works, and my soul knows it very well. My frame was not hidden from You when I was being formed in secret and intricately and skillfully formed [as if embroidered with many colors] in the depths of the earth. Your eyes have seen my unformed substance; And in Your book were all written the days that were appointed for me, when as yet there was not one of them [even taking shape]. How precious also are Your thoughts to me, O God! How vast is the sum of them? If I could count them, they would

outnumber the sand. When I awake, I am still with You." -Psalm 139

13-18 (NIV)

4. You and your spouse have different assignments. You have been uniquely chosen to complete the mission that God has chosen for you. Take this time to discuss the roles that you will play to enhance the gifts that are already inside of you.

"Where two or three gathers in My name, there I am with them." - Matthew 18:20

Pursuing your passion does not make you selfish. When we allow God's prompting, He helps us walk through each season with peace and perseverance. He helps us balance our lives so that our families are not neglected. He ignites the passion that we have for our spouses and shows us how to love them in new ways. While our assignments may be different, when we come together, we create a masterpiece.

War Cry

Lord, help us work together. Give us your wisdom and understanding to complete the assignments you have given us. Send other couples our way to sharpen us when we fall short. Have your way in us, In Jesus' name.
Amen.

Scripture Study

Psalm 57:2, Colossians 1:16, Jeremiah 29:11,

Jeremiah 32:19, Job 42:2, Psalm 33:11, Proverbs 19:21

Chapter 6

Stand Strong

Read Chapter six of Anchored before answering the questions below.

"Many different attacks are coming against families today. It has come to my attention that the enemy is attacking marriages by first attacking the mind of the people involved. "

I've worked in the social service field for many years. One of the things that I've noticed is the lack of knowledge of the enemy's tricks. The most common mental health diagnoses that I've seen are depression and anxiety. They sneak in so suddenly that you don't even realize what is happening. The enemy uses the same old tricks to keep you from reaching your destiny. As I mentioned earlier, he already lost. To win the battle, we must remain armored up. We must use Ephesians 6:10-13 (AMP) as our guide.

"In conclusion, be strong in the Lord [draw your strength from Him and be empowered through your union with Him] and in the power of His [boundless] might. Put on the full armor of God [for His precepts are like the splendid armor of a heavily armed soldier], so that you may

be able to [successfully] stand up against all the schemes and the strategies and the deceits of the devil. For our struggle is not against flesh and blood [contending only with physical opponents], but against the rulers, against the powers, against the world forces of this [present] darkness, against the spiritual forces of wickedness in the heavenly (supernatural) places. Therefore, put on the complete armor of God, so that you will be able to [successfully] resist and stand your ground in the evil day [of danger], and having done everything [that the crisis demands], to stand firm [in your place, fully prepared, immovable, victorious]. "

1. I want you to get a clear picture of the enemy's purpose. He comes ONLY to steal, kill, and destroy. He came so he can ruin everything that comes into your life. He not only wants you, but he also wants your family, your job, your finances etc. DON'T GIVE IT TO HIM!!! Make up in your mind right now that you will not give up without a fight. Think and pray about these things.

2. Is there anything that God has been saying to you repeatedly? What has been your response?

_____

_____

_____

_____

_____

"I am a firm believer that if God continues to repeat something to you, it's time to do something with that information. God is trying to tell you that it's time to put it into practice. It's time not just to hear the word but to be doers of the word also. "

3. What are some tactics that you feel the enemy is using to cause confusion in your home? Take this time to call him out. Let him know who you are and Whose you are.

_____

_____

_____

_____

_____

Taking care of your mental health is a practical way for you to combat the enemy. Most people don't like to talk about mental health, but the truth is understanding your mental health is a necessity. Untreated mental health issues can cause severe problems in your household. It makes you a prime candidate for an attack of the enemy.

4. Take this time and do a self-assessment. Are there areas in your life that depression and anxiety have crept in? Ask God to show you what to do to destroy it.

_____

_____

_____

_____

_____

"Effective communication causes you and your spouse to listen to each other without reacting. It encourages you to listen to the Holy Spirit first before responding to each other."

"Understand this, my beloved brothers and sisters, Let everyone be quick to hear [be a careful and thoughtful listener], slow to speak, [a speaker of carefully chosen words], and slow to anger [patient, reflective, forgiving]." James 1:19

To stand against all the tricks of the enemy, we must armor up. We must protect our legacy. Every generational curse stops with you. When you stand, you shield your family from the enemy's tricks. Make up in your mind today that you will not be shaken.

War Cry

Lord, help us to remain unshakeable. Thank you, Lord God, that we will set an example to our children and destroy every generational curse that has attached itself to our family. Use us for Your glory. In Jesus' name.
Amen.

Scripture Study

I Corinthians 15:58, 1 Timothy 6:12, Luke 21:19.

Philippians 4:13, James 1:2-4, James 4:7

Chapter 7

Be Still

Read Chapter seven of Anchored before answering the questions below.

"Post this at all the intersections, dear friends. Lead with your ears, follow up with your tongue, and let anger straggle along in the rear. God's righteousness doesn't grow from human anger. So, throw all spoiled virtue and cancerous evil in the garbage. In simple humility, let your Gardner (God), landscape you with the word, making a salvation garden of your life."

-James 1:19 (MSG)

Often, when disagreements occur, I find that their emotions are taking the lead. We forget to listen to the heart of a person and react based on our assumptions.

1. When disagreements occur, do you find yourself to be reactive or empathetic? If reactive, what aspect of God's character can you rely on in those moments?

_____

_____

_____

_____

_____

In the beginning, God took his time and created everything just the way He wanted it. When He finished, He called everything good. Not only was it perfect, but it was made to function according to His purpose. Everything was validated by God. We live in a society that is moved by others' opinions instead of God's opinion of us. God is the I Am. He is everything we need Him to be in each moment of our day.

God's love for us is unconditional. That means it is without conditions. You don't have to be good enough, pretty enough, or successful enough to obtain it. It's already ours.

2. What are you allowing to lead your decisions in your relationship?

_____

_____

_____

_____

_____

3. If you are moving in the direction of leaving your relationship, take this time to go deeper with your spouse about the things you feel are causing you to lean towards divorce. What are some things that you feel need to change? Have an honest dialogue with each other. Remember to be quick to hear and slow to speak. Listen to each other's heart and DON'T ASSUME THE WORST!!

"When we allow God to be the master gardener over our lives, He is able to produce the harvest within us. He is the I AM. While our situation may seem unrepairable, it's not too big for Him. Be still and let Him till the soil. Be obedient when He passes you the shovel."

War Cry

Lord, I surrender all and give you control.
Thank you for taking the lead in our relationship.
We have done it our way so many times and failed.
We release our will to yours.
Have your way in us. In Jesus' name.
Amen.

Scripture Study

Exodus 14:14, Psalm 46:10-11, Mark 4:39-41, Psalm 46: 1-3

Chapter 8

Know your Adversary

Read chapter eight of anchored before answering the questions below.

"To keep Satan from taking advantage of us; for we are not ignorant of his schemes." -2 Corinthians 2:11 (AMP)

We have an adversary whose sole purpose is to steal, kill, and destroy. He will do whatever he can to accomplish this. It won't always be noticeable at first. Remember, he uses the same tricks consistently. It may come in the form of depression, anxiety, low self-esteem, people-pleasing, etc. It could show up in unhealthy communication, finances, or your job. Remember that he only has the power that we give him. If I find myself confused or uncertain about an issue, I go back to 1 Corinthians 14:13, which states,

"For God is not the author of confusion, but of peace, as in all the churches of the saints. (NKJV)."

In other words, God didn't write that story. If there is confusion in your household, then you know who the author is. Call him out. Then ask God to give you the wisdom to work it out with your spouse.

1. Identify the tricks that the enemy uses in your relationship.

_____

_____

_____

_____

_____

"Our adversary knows what our hot buttons are. He must know them to be able to do his job. In the same sense, God knows what our cool buttons are. He must know them to be able to do His job."

2. Generational curses were discussed in a previous chapter. What I want you to do here is think about other family members with relationship issues. Do you find a common trend that could be detrimental to your relationship? If so, make up in your mind today that it ends with you. Discuss them with your spouse. This may be a touchy subject. Take some time to pray and ask God to give you the words to speak. Trust Him for His wisdom during your conversation.

"Let's just be candid. Marriage is hard. It's great to have someone to grow old with and snuggle with, but marriage is hard. Bringing together two people with two different personalities and different lifestyles is hard. Add making them one with their own purposes and plans from God, now that's a lot more to think about."

3. Understanding who you are requires you to know whose you are. Take this time to search through the bible and find out what God says about you. Don't be afraid to use the index or the table of contents. The more you know, the more you grow.

    Copy a scripture that you found meaningful.

    _____

    _____

    _____

    _____

    _____

"When we don't know our adversary, we don't know how he will attack. It leaves room for us to respond to our emotions and divorce prematurely."

WAR CRY

Devil, we put you on notice; you cannot have our marriage. You cannot have our family. You cannot have our minds or our finances. Our hearts and our minds belong to Jesus. What God has joined together, no one will separate. NOT EVEN YOU!!!!! God, we ask for a hedge of protection over our marriage. We thank you for your wisdom in remaining focused. Thank you for the eyes to see confusion before it enters our home. In Jesus' name.
Amen.

Scripture Study

Isaiah 40:31, Ephesians 6:12, John 10:10,

Exodus 14:13, 1 Samuel 12:16

Chapter 9

Anchored: Stay the Fight

Read chapter nine of anchored before answering the questions below.

To obey is better than sacrifice, and to heed is better than the fat of rams. -1 Samuel 15:22 (NIV)

Some of us may not have had the best father figure. So, to see God as your father might not be appealing to you. Then to add obedience to the mix may just turn you off completely. If this is the case for you, know that God understands. He is a gentleman and will not force you to do anything you are not ready to do; He will wait for you. When the enemy comes to do his job, God will walk beside you and wait for you to surrender it all to Him. He will comfort you as you walk out your journey. When you are ready, He will be waiting for you with open arms.

1. What memories do you have of your biological father? If the memories you have are negative, do you find it harder to believe that God is who He says He is?

   _____

   _____

   _____

_____

_____

2. How important is it to lay the foundation in your marriage during the dating stage? If you are already married, did you skip this step? Why or why not?

_____

_____

_____

_____

_____

"In laying the foundation for our marriage, Kevin and I vowed to base our marriage off of three pillars: communication, accountability, and prayer. Anytime the enemy tried to cause confusion in our home, we would go back to these three pillars."

3. How could these three pillars be beneficial in your home?

_____

_____

_____

_____

_____

Remember to laugh together. In marriage, your friendship must come before your relationship. You don't want to marry someone just to have someone to snuggle with. You marry in hopes that you will grow old together. Proverbs 17:22 (AMP) tells us,

"A happy heart is good medicine, and a joyful mind causes healing, but a broken spirit dries up the bones."

4. Laughter is healthy. It helps you grow through the groanings. When is the last time you laughed together? Do you feel like you married your best friend? Why or why not? If not, take this time to plan out a date and get to know each other again.

_____

_____

_____

_____

_____

"To be anchored in your marriage is to be fixed to prevent you and your spouse from moving from that place. To be anchored means to remain despite your feelings, emotions, backgrounds, family history, and the issues plaguing our society. To be anchored means to bloom where you are planted. Marriage is no easy road, but with the right tools and determination to stay in the fight, it is well worth it."

WAR CRY

Lord, our hope is in you. In the trials and tribulations of life, we know that you are working behind the scenes. You are the author and finisher of our faith. We look to you acknowledging where our help comes from. In Jesus' name.
Amen.

Scripture Study

Hebrews 6:19, Psalm 11:3, Isaiah 26:3, Psalm 25:5,

Isaiah 28:16, Psalm 62:5

Scan here to check out my blogs, videos, and podcasts. If you like what you've read, I would really appreciate it if you left a review.

71% of young ladies aging out of foster care will become pregnant by the age of 21.

Imagine being taken from your home and the only family you've ever known, your brothers, sisters, mom, and dad. You wonder where you are going. Who is going to take care of you? What is going to happen to your siblings? Who is going to take care of them? Regardless of the reasoning for being placed in foster care, you long to be with your family. Time passes, and you are almost at the point where you can age out of the system. By this time, you've burned many bridges, missed out on a lot of education, and lack the necessary life skills needed to be successful. Your eighteenth birthday is approaching quickly, but you have no skills and no family to turn to. What will you do?

At The Family Connection Inc., Our mission is to assist children who are aging out of foster care with the tools to become self-sufficient. We will teach them life skills, offer them counseling services, case management, educational development, and career guidance. They will have the opportunity to transition into their own living space with their case management team's help. Our vision is to equip families and individuals with the necessary resources for success.

For more information go to www.familyconnectioninc.org

Page 53 of 53

Made in the USA
Columbia, SC
19 November 2023

26468011R00033